Other booklets in the Affirming Catholicism series

AFFIRMING CATHOLICISM

Jane Williams

TRINITY
AND
UNITY

DARTON·LONGMAN+TODD

JANE WILLIAMS read theology at Cambridge and now works as an editor for Darton, Longman and Todd. She was on a British Council of Churches commission on the Doctrine of the Trinity and is the co-author of *Bread, Wine and Women* (with Susan Dowell, Virago, 1994).

© Jane Williams 1995

Published by Darton, Longman and Todd, 1 Spencer Court,
140–142 Wandsworth High Street, London SW18 4JJ
in association with Affirming Catholicism, St Mary-le-Bow,
Cheapside, London EC2V 6AU

ISBN 0–232–52137–9

The views expressed in this booklet are those of the
author and do not necessarily reflect any policy
of Affirming Catholicism.

Booklets designed by Bet Ayer, phototypeset by Intype, London
and printed by Halstan and Co Ltd, Amersham, Bucks

CONTENTS

Affirming Catholicism

Affirming Catholicism has never been, and is not intended to be, yet another 'party' within the Church of England or the Anglican Communion but rather a movement of encouragement and hope.

A group of lay people and clergy met together in 1990 to identify that authentic Catholic tradition within the Church which appeared to be under threat. Wider support was expressed at a public meeting on 9 June 1990 in London and at a residential conference in York in July 1991.

Since then Affirming Catholicism has been afforded charitable status. The following statement is extracted from the Trust Deed:

> It is the conviction of many that a respect for scholarship and free enquiry has been character-istic of the Church of England and of the Churches of the wider Anglican Communion from earliest times and is fully consistent with the status of those Churches as part of the Holy Catholic Church. It is desired to establish a charitable educational foundation which will be true both to those characteristics and to the Catholic tradition within Anglicanism ... The object of the foundation shall be the advancement of education in the doctrines and the historical development of the Church of England and the Churches of the wider Anglican Communion, as held by those professing to stand within the Catholic tradition.

In furtherance of these aims and objectives, Affirming Catholicism is producing this series of booklets. The series will encompass two sets of books: one set will attempt to present a clear, well-argued Catholic viewpoint on issues of debate facing the Church at any given time; the other set will cover traditional doctrinal themes. The editor of the series is Jeffrey John; the other titles in the series are listed at the front of this booklet.

To order these publications individually or on subscription, or for enquiries regarding the aims and activities of Affirming Catholicism write to:

The Secretary
Mainstream
St Mary-le-Bow
Cheapside
London EC2V 6AU

Tel: 0171–329 4070

TRINITY
AND
UNITY

Introduction

In times past the doctrine of the Trinity has sometimes appeared as the kind of mad relation beloved of Victorian authors. It was generally kept locked up in the attic, but occasionally escaped to alarm the unsuspecting visitor. Perhaps the overwhelming impression given by most writers on the Trinity is that it is something *extra*, to be added to the essential doctrines of Christology.[1] After all, the formularies about who Christ is and what he does have clear biblical bases, and the relationship between Christ and the Father can be pictured in ways that appeal to the imagination, as is clear from centuries of Christian art. Look at the number of pictures that depict Christ and the Father but forget about the Spirit.

So the doctrine of the Trinity comes to be seen as a latecomer in doctrinal terms, one with dubious biblical backing, that has to be formulated in abstract mathematical and philosophical language that is distinctly uninspiring. Even when duty compels treatment of Trinitarian theology in systematic works that cover Christian doctrine, the fire has generally gone out of the writers' pens by the time they move on from Christ to the Spirit.[2]

But in the last decade or so, this seems to have changed. Books on the Trinity proliferate, and the doctrine seems to have been dragged from the attic into the living room and set to solve all the difficult questions that other doctrinal speculation leaves untouched. In particular, modern writers have fallen upon the doctrine of the Trinity as a way of addressing pressing theological questions about community, about the formation of persons, about God's continuing presence in the world and in the Church, and about how men and women should relate in God's world. Rather a tall order, you might imagine, and certainly, as we shall see, not all the solutions that emerge are properly *Trinitarian*, nor do they always offer the answers they promise, but it does lead us to ask how the doctrine of the Trinity gained this new prominence.

Two great and unrelated movements seem to lie at the heart of the rediscovery of the Trinity among Western theologians. One is the ecumenical movement, which brought Western church people into contact with the much richer Trinitarian theology of the Eastern orthodox churches.[3] The other is the charismatic movement. By emphasizing the work of the Spirit and the gifts of the Spirit, the charismatic movement has helped to remind the Western church that the Spirit, like the Father and the Son, is *personal*. Within the charismatic movement the Holy Spirit is not the abstract third term, the gooseberry between the Father and the Son, the one who has to be found little jobs to do to justify its existence, but one whose part in God's plan of salvation is as clear and necessary as those of Father and Son.

In this booklet, the intention is to look briefly at some of the history of the doctrine of the Trinity, then to move on to a survey of some significant shifts in modern writing on the Trinity, and lastly to suggest pointers for future thought and work.

The doctrine of the Trinity – Historical Perspectives

Defining the doctrine

It is perfectly true that the doctrine of the Trinity is not to be found in the Bible. Nowhere does the Bible say that Christ is 'of one being (*homoousios*) with the Father', nor does it say that the three persons of the Godhead exist in three hypostases but share one *ousia*. These are the technical terms of later patristic definitions. But they were not invented out of nothing and for the love of complications. They were hammered out with great arguments about the nature both of the biblical witness and of accepted church practice, and the exact, almost mathematical, formulations that were finally agreed upon were thought to be the ones that best defined Christian experience of Father, Son and Spirit, in the past and in the present.

Christian writers of the first few centuries did not have to defend the notion of the existence of God, as they would have to today, but they did have to work hard to justify calling Son and Spirit 'God', too. For the first few hundred years, Christian theological controversy largely centred round the question of the relationship between Jesus Christ and the God whom he called 'Father'. Many who were quite prepared to acknowledge Jesus' uniqueness saw no reason to make the next leap and call him 'God'. Many others agreed that Jesus was the embodiment of the divine *Logos*, but were not sure how that affected his humanity. Was he merely a human outer casing with a divine motivating force, or was he two complete beings, one human, one divine, somehow cohabiting in the one human form of Jesus?[4] These controversies spawned many heresies, which came to their official resolution at the councils of Nicaea (325) and Chalcedon (451), although debate continues to this day. The council of Nicaea used the word '*homoousios*' to describe how Father and Son are related. It is usually translated 'of one being or substance', and was intended to rule out the notion that Jesus was merely a unique but created being. Instead, it emphasizes that Jesus is like the Father, as no creature is, and that his existence is intrinsic to that of the Father, not something additional or externally caused.

The definition was hotly debated, as was the use of the non-biblical word '*homoousios*'. Its defenders had to argue that only this word could do full justice to the biblical witness and to continuing Christian experience of salvation and recreation through Christ. In particular, one of its defenders, Gregory of Nazianzus, made it clear that our salvation is *dependent* upon Jesus being God incarnate. 'What was not assumed was not healed', he argued. In other words, if Jesus was not fully human and fully God, then our own human nature is not redeemed by the recreative power of God at work within it.

The council of Chalcedon in 451 reaffirmed this definition by stating emphatically that Jesus is both fully human and fully divine and that the two natures exist 'without confusion, without change, without division and without separation'.

Clearly, none of this is read directly out of the New Testament, though at each stage it was justified in relation to a reading of the New Testament. It was also justified in relation to accepted Christian practice – what do we think we are *doing* when we pray through Christ, and when we receive the Eucharistic elements as his body and blood 'given for our salvation'? It is important to understand that what emerges as a complicated philosophical definition comes by way of Christian experience and devotional practice.

The same can be said of the next stage of the Trinitarian process in relation to the Holy Spirit. During the centuries in which debate was concentrated on Christological controversies, the Trinity was not absent from Christian writing and practice. Like the developed doctrine of Christ, so the developed doctrine of the Trinity is not worked out in the New Testament, but references to Father, Son and Holy Spirit are clearly part of Christian language and liturgical practice in our earliest records.[5] Even before the full definition of the doctrine, Christian writers were commending the Trinity to their congregations in various images; Irenaeus (second century), for example, speaks of the Son and the Spirit as the two hands of God.

Problems continued to arise about the exact relationship between the persons of the Trinity, and these problems were not merely abstractions. Origen, for example, was concerned about how we should direct our prayers. Should we pray equally to all three persons of the Trinity, just to the Father, or to 'God', implying always to all three together? Origen concluded that prayer should properly be directed only to the Father, though this does not imply that Son and Spirit are not involved with the process of our prayer. In practice, Origen's view has largely won in traditional liturgy. If you look, for example, at the Anglican Eucharistic liturgy, prayer is addressed to the Father, so that it is usual to use some such formula as 'to the Father, through the Son, in the Spirit', to describe the Trinitarian process of prayer. I suspect that private prayer does not always follow this practice, particularly for those praying in traditions where either Jesus or the Spirit have centrality.

When the definition of Jesus' divinity became largely accepted, it was clearly necessary to argue the equal divinity of the Spirit, if the Spirit's role as part of the process of salvation was to be safeguarded. The exact definition of the relations of the three persons of the Trinity is usually ascribed largely to the work of the Cappadocian Fathers, Basil the Great, Gregory of Nazianzus and Gregory of Nyssa. They argued that the persons of the Trinity are three, but that they share the same 'substance' (*ousia*). So they can be distinguished from each other in their relations – the Father is not the Son, the Son is not the Spirit; the Father is the Father of the Son, and so on – and, to some extent, they can be distinguished by their activity – neither the Father nor the Spirit dies upon the cross – but they are indistinguishable in their nature and their will – they are all God, they are all love, they are all involved in salvation and recreation.

Splitting the Church – the 'filoque' controversy

It seems ironic that this great definition of the persons of the Godhead at work in creation and recreation should have provided the excuse for fragmenting the church. St Augustine is usually blamed for this, as for most things that went wrong in Western theology.[6] Actually, of course, his theology articulates something that was being said by many others, and was simply a part of the process of defining how the persons of the Trinity relate to each other.

Augustine is credited with having popularized the idea that Anglicans now express Sunday by Sunday when we say the Creed; when we come, rather tardily, to the Holy Spirit at the end of the Creed, we say that the Holy Spirit proceeds 'from the Father *and the Son*'. In other words, we seem to be saying that the relation of the Holy Spirit to the Father is mediated by the Son, rather than being as direct as the Son's own. The Latin for 'and the Son' is *'filioque'*, and it is from this Latin that the controversy that split the Eastern and Western churches is named.

Now, of course, that split was not *just* about theology – what split ever is? It was also about the increasing dominance of the papacy, about the treachery of the West during the crusades and all manner of other political things. But by the eleventh and twelfth centuries, Eastern and Western churches were in a state of bitter hostility and schism, to the point where a Patriarch of Constantinople, Michael Anchialus (1169–1177), thought that it would be better to be conquered by the Muslims – a very real possibility at the time – than to be forced to accept the faith of the West.

To split the Church over two words seems absurd, and the majority of theologians, Eastern and Western, would now be happy to drop the *'filioque'*, and substitute a phrase like 'proceeds from the Father *with* the Son', which would seem to satisfy all the necessary Trinitarian considerations. But though it is easy for us to see that such a compromise is good and necessary, there were actually some real theological issues behind the original split.

One was the attempt to be faithful to the biblical witness. Western theologians argued that, particularly in the letter of St Paul and in the Gospel of John, the work of the Spirit is clearly Christ-shaped and the coming of the Spirit seems to be in the gift of Jesus. Look, for example, at Romans 8.15–17 'When we cry "Abba! Father!" it is the Spirit himself bearing witness . . . that we are . . . fellow heirs with Christ'. The Spirit's job is to make us able to stand in Jesus' own place in relation to the Father. Or, look at John 14.16 'And I will pray the Father and he will give you another Counsellor, to be with you for ever, even the Spirit of truth'. But equally, one could find biblical verses that suggest a very different picture; the Luke-Acts record, for example, has a highly distinctive understanding of the work of the Holy Spirit, which forms the basis for much charismatic pneumatology.

The Western understanding of the place of the Spirit has two really damaging consequences, for which theology at large had continued to pay the price. The first is that, by focussing on the relationship of the Father and the Son, and making the Spirit a mere by-product, the figure of the Spirit becomes vague and insubstantial. The extent to which the Spirit failed to find an imaginative role in Western art is clear in all those pictures of two men and a bird. Compare that with Rublev's mysterious and lovely Trinity of equal persons grouped around the table. From the time when Augustine described the Holy Spirit as the 'bond of love' between Father and Son, it is clear that theologians have been having a struggle to find something for the poor old Spirit to do, and certainly the notion of the spirit as fully personal, like the Father and the Son, far too easily vanishes.

The other drawback of this way of thinking of the Spirit is that it undermines the whole point of Trinitarian theology. The basis of our understanding of God as Trinity is that God's own nature is one of self-giving love. God is constituted, not by being 'one is one and all alone and ever more shall be so', but by being in relation. God relates, even before we exist to be related to. The Cappadocian Fathers, who gave us the classic, pre-schism definition of the Trinity were clear that the words we have to describe how God relates to God are *just that and no more*. They are terms that describe the relationship, and not necessarily exact descriptions. Again, this presents problems in speaking about the Spirit, since 'Father' and 'Son' are clearly relational terms – you don't get to be a father or a son unless you have someone who is a son or a father – but 'Spirit' is not.

But if the whole point of the exercise is to emphasize that God is wholly relational, then to start niggling about which members of the Godhead relate to which is to drive a wedge through the entire argument. If the Spirit only relates to the Father through the Son, then the Father is so much the less relational.[7] What starts off as part of God's great assurance to us that God is to be loved and approached and trusted degenerates into a kind of mathematical exercise.

In the sections that follow, I want to look at one or two modern developments that are helping to rescue Trinitarian theology from that kind of irrelevance and abstraction, and bring it back where it belongs, as one of the most creative and stimulating ways we have of knowing God.

God with us – Trinitarian theology and Christian experience

Personal and Corporate Experience

One of the most helpful recent trends in Trinitarian theology has been – though I hesitate to use the phrase – the 'back to basics' approach. Where did this doctrine come from, and, more importantly, why?

The impetus behind it was, as we have already seen, the intricate web of scripture, experience and liturgical practice, which all form and are formed by each other. The writers of the New Testament were trying to describe what they and their contemporaries had experienced, and what they were already doing in their public and private praying, even before the documents of the New Testament were produced. Later writers then draw on their own personal experience of God, shaped and translated for them by scripture and by liturgy. So to say that this doctrine is 'experience-based' is not to claim a kind of solipsistic worshipping ego, but to speak of something that is already instinctively communal and that *believes that communality is an expression of the God it worships.*

Liturgy and hymnody, in particular, then become the source books for Trinitarian theology. It is probably much too simplistic to say that as society became more fragmented and individualistic, and less 'catholic', so more emphasis was put on private prayer, and on personal devotion to Jesus, and there were fewer and fewer references to the Trinity in liturgy and in manuals of prayer. It is, for example, interesting to note that the ASB is very largely binitarian, except in the Eucharistic prayer, the Creed and the final blessing.[8] The Orthodox liturgy, on the other hand, constantly calls upon the three-fold name. This may not necessarily reflect any profound grasp upon the doctrine by all Orthodox congregations, but it does suggest a much greater degree of habit and familiarity.

It is also too simplistic, but quite suggestive, to say that many radical groupings within the Church become more profoundly Trinitarian, because if you are looking for a basis on which to found a new, more egalitarian society, the doctrine of the Trinity is a good place to start. As we shall see, Christian feminist groups have made good use of the doctrine of the Trinity for rethinking the relationship between women and men in the Church, and some particularly good Trinitarian hymns and prayers have emerged under this impetus.[9]

Trinitarian prayer
But it is important to emphasize that our liturgical life has a private as well as a public dimension, and that Trinitarian theology arises very directly out of an understanding of what we are doing when we pray, whether that prayer be 'in church' or not. It is a point that is made with particular clarity and force by a chapter in the report of the Church of England's doctrine commission, *We Believe in God*.[10] The author emphasizes things that will be familiar to all Christians who pray, as well as from the vast Christian literature about prayer.

For example, there is the familiar sensation of being 'prayed in', of the presence of the Spirit bringing us to the point where we want to pray and are able to pray, despite the dumbness and unwillingness of our own instincts. This impulse is often almost in spite of ourselves. How often do you hear people say 'something made me fall to my knees?'

And then this first movement begins to take a shape. We begin to find ourselves becoming 'Christ-like'. This is not a claim that all Christians become supernaturally virtuous in prayer, since all the evidence is otherwise. No, to become 'Christ-like' is, initially, to know that we are loved, that we are children of God, 'heirs of the Father, joint heirs with the son'; it is to share Christ's place, the one carved out for us by Christ's Incarnation, and prepared for us by God's first creative act.[11] Above all, it is to be in that special relationship to the God whom Jesus teaches us and the Spirit encourages us to call 'Father'.

The report goes on to point out that since this is *Christian* prayer that we are talking about, prayer in the image of Christ, it should not surprise us that prayer has an element of the cross in it. All the great mystics of the Christian tradition speak of darkness, uncertainty, failure and pain as an inevitable part of prayer. Yet we so often think that prayer is only hard if we are not doing it right. Sometimes, of course, prayer *is* hard because we are not doing it right – and this usually means we are not doing it enough.

But so long as we are there, doing it faithfully and regularly, whatever the boredom and distraction, then we are doing it right. If praying is relational, we should not expect it to be simpler than other relationships. If prayer is Christ-like, we should not expect it to be without the cross.

Prayer is, indeed, centrally relational, and the relationship is not just between the Christian and God-in-Trinity. We are not the only ones in whom the Spirit is making the likeness of the Son of the Father. All around us, the Spirit is creating that likeness, so that, inevitably, Trinitarian prayer is prayer in community. The most solitary hermit prays for others and is joined with them through that prayer. And all of us, through prayer, become part of the Trinitarian life of God. Trinitarian prayer is one of the most profound acknowledgements that that is what the Christian life is about – it is about being taken into God's own life. And that life, so Romans 8 tells us, as does the whole doctrine of creation, encompasses not only us but God's creation in its entirety.

Now, clearly, this account of Trinitarian prayer is shaped by our understanding of the Bible and of our liturgical life. Much of what has been said above could equally well be said of the Eucharist – the indwelling of the Spirit, the Christ-like shaping of our natures, the self-giving of God, the being taken into God's life, the inevitable corporate nature of the act, the transformation of bread and wine, as symbols of inanimate creation, transparent to God's deeper, symbol-working nature.[12]

In other words, this is not 'unmediated' experience of the Trinity. There is, in any case, no such thing as 'unmediated experience' – experience always comes packaged by our preconceptions of what we 'know to be true' – and this argument that the doctrine of the Trinity derives primarily from Christian experience is not intended as an evangelical argument. This will not convert non-Christians to Christianity – though the vision of the Trinitarian God might – but it might convert Christians to a fuller understanding of God, Three in One.

God hidden and God shared

Catherine LaCugna, in her fascinating book *God for Us*,[13] argues that the Church abandoned the doctrine of the Trinity and avoided its radical appeal centuries ago, when theology introduced us to the distinction between the 'immanent' and the 'economic' Trinity. I will explain about that in a minute, but for the moment, let us stick with what LaCugna has to say. 'The doctrine of the trinity is ultimately a practical doctrine with radical consequences for Christian life', she argues on page one of her book.

The starting point of Trinitarian theology, as I have been arguing above, is the experience of God at work to save us. Theologians call this – God at work to save us – the 'economy' of salvation. When the first Christians began to make their extraordinary claims about Jesus Christ, the claims that led to the belief that Jesus is God incarnate, they were saying something very radical about the nature of God. They were saying that the way in which we experience God is *true*. For all the immensity of the gulf between Creator and creatures, for all the inability of the human mind to fathom the divine, nonetheless, the way in which we experience God at work to save us in Jesus is the truth about God's very nature. It is not something that God does every so often. It is not a small aspect of God's activity in the world. It is not just something that we *perceive*, but that will, ultimately, be shown to have some other explanation. On the contrary, it is the revelation of the very nature of God, how God is, whether we are there to see it or not. How God is to Godself is what theologians call the 'immanent' Trinity.

LaCugna argues that, through the Christian centuries, and for various reasons,[14] theologians came to talk more and more of a distinction between the 'economic' and the 'immanent' Trinity, and Trinitarian language became increasingly confined to a kind of grammatical code-language for talking about God-in-and-for-Godself, and increasingly divorced from its roots in the experience of God at work to save us, God, Father, Son and Holy Spirit, combining to lift us into their own loving and self-giving.

LaCugna's book is not without problems, and I want, myself, to defend some of the 'grammatical' points about how we apply language to God, but she does accurately set out how the doctrine of the Trinity has largely been used. She also presents a solution that has proved to be one of the highly attractive developments in modern Trinitarian theology. Theologians as diverse as Rahner and Moltmann have wanted to query the traditional distinction between 'economic' and 'immanent' Trinity.[15] Surely one thing we might guess at about God, from the Incarnation, is that God is not interested in being separate from us and in keeping divine life only for divine persons. The need to protect God from what appear to be God's own acts of self-destructive self-revelation and self-exposure seems to run very deep in us, and LaCugna's insistence that we must let God be God as God chooses to be is surely vital.

Trinitarian Feminism

The vulnerable God

The vulnerable God who is truly involved in creation, and who has no interest in being 'in control' is a God who appeals greatly to feminists. For a long time, so the caricature goes, the main teaching of Christianity was the divinity of hierarchy. It is a caricature, but like all good caricatures, it has enough truth in it to be uncomfortable. The hierarchies within society, the hierarchy within the Church, the hierarchy between men and women, all seemed to reach their justification in a doctrine that suggested there was hierarchy within God's very nature. At the top, in charge, there is the Father, then there is the obedient Son, and from the Son proceeds the Spirit.

But if the Trinity is actually *primarily* about how we experience God at work in saving and recreating us day by day, then the picture is very different. God the Father is content to be familiar to us, content to be described in homely parables, content to be misunderstood by those who were not listening properly or were not very bright or just did not like the sound of it. God the Son is content to be human, to be limited, to be vulnerable, to die, God the Spirit is content to teach our stumbling tongues to pray 'Father', to work in the tiny chinks we allow for the upbuilding of the Church, to go unremarked and unrecognized in the saints whom most of us ignore most of the time. What has all this to do with hierarchy, with control, with power?

Actually, of course, it has everything to do with power, but a power too frightening for most of us to cope with most of the time. It is a power I saw at work, for example, in the great Dutch Reformed resistor of apartheid, Beyers Naude, who was imprisoned, kept away from all meetings, confined to his house for years. And in many of the other great leaders of the fight against apartheid in South Africa. I remember one man, who had been imprisoned and tortured and betrayed, saying 'if they have done all that, and still they have not broken you, then they know they are powerless, and you have won!' The one unbeatable power is that which never gives up and never allows violence to change its nature. That is one small glimpse of what God's understanding of power might be.

Of course, we must not sentimentalize this power. It is also the power that made the world out of nothing, that made the whirlwind and the tempest as well as the sun and the rainbow. It is also the power that is markedly not used to save what it loves from all suffering. If it is anarchic, levelling, never-ending, it is also mysterious and terrifying. Christmas and the cross, resurrection and the end of the world.

Sorry, where was I? Oh, yes, Trinity and feminism. Feminism has sometimes tended to talk about the radical, egalitarian, ecological vision of society which can be drawn from our understanding of Trinitarian love as the basis of the world without also being willing to look at the cost. For example, Sallie McFague wrote a highly influential book called *Models of God* in which she suggests that the model of the world as God's body should become a primary way of talking about how God and the world relate.[16] But in so doing she seems to suggest that the ravaged and ravaging nature of this 'body' is not theologically serious, but some accident that will be taken care of when we come to accept the model properly. But the ravaged body on the cross suggests that the whole problem is more complex than that. We do not, and we *cannot by ourselves* accept any models that lead to our salvation.

The sex of God?

Some feminist writing has assumed that if we can suggest that some part of the Trinity is feminine, then we have gone a long way towards solving the problem of sexism. After all, did not Mary Daly famously say that 'where God is male, the male is God'?

The person of the Trinity usually chosen to be female is the Holy Spirit. This is partly because 'Father' and 'Son' seem rather conclusively male names, and partly because the Hebrew word for 'Spirit', '*ruach*', is a feminine noun, and partly, I suspect, because the Holy Spirit seems such a nice, co-operative sort of soul, working with people to build up things and so forth (but don't forget the tongues of flame).

Although this can prove a very useful first step, encouraging people to think about 'feminine' qualities associated with God, and leading them on gently to think about complementarity and co-creativeness, it can leave the actual state of relationships between women and men quite unchanged, and the stereotypes of 'male' and 'female' unchallenged. Too often, the feminine Holy Spirit is characterized by intuitive, sensitive, nurturing qualities, the ones that women are supposed to possess, the ones that are supposed to prevent them from wanting to manage their business, or become priests or stand up for their rights. The dangers of this approach become clear if you read a book like Leonardo Boff's *The Maternal Face of God*.[17] This is supposed to be a very radical book, in that it suggests that the Virgin Mary is the incarnation of the Holy Spirit. It might be theologically radical, but it is not radical for women, since this 'incarnation' is characterized by receptivity and passivity (markedly different from the Son's incarnation).

Nor does it necessarily achieve anything for the feminist cause to call the first person of the Trinity 'the motherly Father'. Again, this is to value as 'feminine' precisely the qualities that have always stereotypically belonged to women. But it is not necessarily to value them *in women*, but only when grafted onto the male. Nor does the obvious next step take place, which might be to value 'fatherly mothers'. So in fact, what starts off as a promising sounding avenue for seeing the feminine side of God quickly becomes just another colonization of the female by the male. It seems that maleness can even encompass femaleness better than females can.

Unless the 'feminine' God is one who empowers women and enables them to be themselves in relation to men and to each other, rather than living by some preordained stereotype of 'womanhood', then whether God is 'she' or 'he' makes no difference. After all, we have no evidence that societies that worship female deities actually treat women any better. So it would seem that Mary Daly's famous dictum needs to be altered slightly, to say that where God is a dictator, of whatever sex, then women will be dictated to.

But women are surely right to scent in the doctrine of the Trinity something important for the cause of freedom. That something is not the sex of God, however. That is one of the useful 'grammatical' points that the arid-sounding theologists of the Middle Ages made. God does not have a sex because God does not have a body, except, of course, the Church. God has qualities that our society describes variously as 'male' and 'female', but the most basic study of anthropology will make it clear that the majority of these qualities are socially-shaped, not innate. So theologies that attempt to find 'masculine' qualities and 'feminine' qualities in God are groping their way towards the far more important assertion that each of us shows some spark of God's own love, and that, like all love, it can only be seen, only make sense, within the context of a *relationship*.

The social Trinity

The doctrine of the Trinity, with all the different ways in which it is taken up and described in the New Testament and subsequent writings, offers many examples of just what that might mean in practice. Above all the doctrine of the Trinity offers an idea of a *society*, in which persons are shaped by relation and interaction, in which each is anxious only to discover the full depths of the other, and to point them out for the rest of the society. All of Paul's passages about 'the body' come to mind here, the body that has need of every part, where there is no sense in talking about which is better than the other, since all are necessary, where there can be no talk of dominance and submission, since all work together as an organic whole.

That, surely, is a vision that Christian feminists might espouse? It does not commit us to undue meekness, since if you are called to be part of the body, you know you are necessary, and it is no good someone telling you to be a rhododendron instead. It is true that believing in the Trinity also commits you to working for unity, but it has to be a truthful unity. You cannot unite 'yourself' with another if you have already abandoned any attempt to be 'yourself'. The members of the Trinity each take as their work to point to the others and to create the place where the others may be seen and recognized and grow, and yet they remain distinct in unity. The Father does not become the Son, nor the Son the Spirit, and it is in preserving the distinctions in their relations that they create the place where the others can come too. The Spirit is apprehended by us precisely in performing the acts that shape Christ in us, and yet these acts are distinctive to the Spirit.

Inevitably, when one starts to talk like this, it is hard not to make the persons of the Trinity sound like a particularly slick football team. To dwell on the different persons seems to put too much emphasis upon their 'threeness' rather than their 'oneness', and yet even the threeness presses towards unity, presses towards the time when we, too, shall be taken up into that life that is both so diverse and yet so concentrated. Unity is always the aim of Trinitarian theology, the unity of all persons in Christ, the unity of Father, Son and Holy Spirit, the unity of all creation. But if we take the Trinity seriously, we are at liberty to believe that unity need not mean the end of distinctions, but might actually lead us to value our distinctions more, that it might actually be possible to reach a point where differences bring us close together, where unity is achieved by acknowledging that we have need of each other. 'We are to grow up in every way into him who is the head, into Christ, from whom the whole body, joined and knit together by every joint with which it is supplied, when each part is working properly, makes bodily growth and upbuilds itself in love' (Eph 4.15–16).

Conclusion

In God's image: what it means to be a person
The Orthodox tradition has often accused the West of placing so much emphasis on God's unity that we forget God's Trinity. But, inevitably, when you concentrate on the Trinity, there is a strong temptation to make God sound like three 'people'. They may be unusually close, and share a strong family resemblance, but they are still three, and they are still 'persons'.

In much of what I have already written, I suspect that I have fallen into that trap. The trap has all kinds of advantages, in that it retains the familiar emphasis on God as personal and loving, while yet remaining social rather than individualistic. Many theologians now want to emphasize that, for good or ill, people are only formed *in relationships*. Personality is not something that comes out of nowhere, but it is created through interaction with others.

And, again, it is all too easy to make a quick leap from that to its foundation and ground in God's own nature. God, too, is persons formed in and through relationships, and so God in Trinity is the most satisfying image we have of how persons should be made and how societies should function.

That is an important insight, not to be lightly abandoned. But it is just as important to remember that God is equally properly described as Three and as One. We are not.

Although it is quite right and proper to ground our knowledge of how human beings should relate and grow in community in our understanding of God's own loving and self-giving nature, it is equally important to remember that the truth that those words express is only approximate. Thomas Aquinas, who did the classic groundwork on how language can and cannot be used in relation to God, is clear that only abstract nouns apply to God without qualification. So it is absolutely true to say that God is love, but it is analogically true to say that God is Father. In other words, the latter has the truth and force of a particularly appropriate picture, but it is not true in every detail, whereas there is nothing about God that is unloving, and no circumstances in which that would be an inappropriate description of God.

The language about 'personhood' in relation to God is, I suspect, in the same category as 'Fatherhood', rather than 'Love'. God is not 'a person', in the sense that we are, or even 'three persons'. God's personality does not grow and change in relation to others, God's emotional state is not determined by others and so on. It is sometimes helpful sometimes unhelpful to think of God as a person.

Like the language of 'Father' and 'Son' in relation to God, the language of 'personhood' has a strong claim on the Christian imagination because of the Incarnation, when God became, indeed, a person, as we are. It also makes sense of a particularly fruitful line of Christian theology, which starts with our creation 'in God's image', and progresses through Isaiah's 'suffering servant' imagery until it arrives at St Paul's 'First' and 'Last' Adam metaphor. All of this concerns the purpose of our human existence and God's continued faithfulness to us. We are created to know God and to show God, and we continue to do that, by God's grace, throughout God's redeeming history with us. Jesus is what we were made to be, and in recognizing Jesus as God's image, we are, at the same time, recognizing our true selves. This spark of recognition, this extraordinary knowledge that we are made to be like God, is God's great gift to us, offered again and again in creation and recreation, and it would be false modesty to reject it and put all the emphasis instead upon our difference from God, how unlike God we are.

This is another one of those instances where Trinitarian language is usefully mind-boggling. You have to be able to say *both* that we are like God *and* that God is not like us. Just as Trinitarian language reminds us of the inexact status of the language of 'Father', and 'Son' in relation to God, so it also reminds us that it is both necessary and unsatisfactory to think of God as 'a person'. The Trinity is both an image of personhood on which we know that we are, by our creation, modelled, and it is also a mathematical device for reminding us that we are made in God's image, not God in ours.

Confirming the Incarnation

We have seen in the course of this booklet that the major deathblow to the doctrine of the Trinity was to sever it from its natural place in the saving work of God. If the Trinity is thought of as something 'extra', something perhaps that God knows about God but that is of little obvious relevance to us, then we have missed one of the most fruitful ways we have of seeing God at work.

At its most basic, the doctrine of the Trinity confirms what is clear from the Incarnation. It is not something over and above the Incarnation, something without which the Incarnation would work anyway, but part and parcel of the same great act of creation and recreation, of self-giving and salvation, which has been God's work from the beginning.

The Incarnation, we are told, shows us God's loving and self-giving nature, but it should also remind us that this is what God has *always* been like. It should encourage us to look around for other signs of that same nature at work. The very existence of creation shows it, as does creation's independence from its creator. Although in one sense it is religiously-speaking important to emphasize the astonishing fact that *God* became *human*, and to remember the aweful self-emptying involved in that, Trinitarian theology reminds us that there is another side to this. This one great act of God in the Incarnation is also part of God's continuing movement to be relational, to be shown in variety and distinction, as well as in unity and synthesis.

The Incarnation shows us that human nature can be transparent to God, and that God constantly recreates so that the original creative impulse 'to make man in his own image' is never lost. Yet, without something very like the doctrine of the Trinity, it is hard to see how that helps us. If Jesus is just an example to us, then we have had it. The example of goodness has always existed in human beings, here and there, and most of us have proved perfectly able to resist its lure. But Trinitarian theology assures us that God does not come among us, die, rise and then sit up above and watch how we get on. On the contrary, that desire on God's part to *be with us* is constant, as it has always been. The Holy Spirit continues to work with us and in us and for us to bring God's creation to fulfilment.

In other words, Trinitarian theology makes it clear to us that the doctrines of creation and salvation are recognizably made of the same cloth, the cloth of God's loving, multi-faceted nature. It also makes it clear why we say that the crucifixion is about love. For years I found the words 'God so loved the world that he gave his only-begotten son' problematic. What kind of love did this show, and did I, as a representative of 'the world' want to be loved like that? It sounded to me suspiciously like the same kind of love that said 'I could not love thee, dear, so much, loved I not honour more'. And that is the kind of love that has always been used to justify men doing what they want to do and leaving the women behind holding the children. Was that

God's kind of love? The kind that was prepared to sacrifice the person it loved for some supposedly greater good?

The problem became more severe for me after I had a child of my own, and I knew for certain that *under no circumstances whatsoever* would I sacrifice her for the greater good. E M Forster said 'If I had the choice between betraying my friend and betraying my country, I hope I would have the courage to betray my country', and I entirely sympathized with him. It is very easy, and Christians have been particularly prone, to talk about 'love' in the abstract, but to neglect the love of the particular, the person you are actually given to love.

But this way of looking at the love of God, which makes God the stern but actually unloving headmaster-figure, is one of those dangerous spin-offs of talking about our relationship to God exclusively in Father/child imagery. In fact, the kind of love shared between Father and Son is not where the Father tells the son what to do, but one where there is a shared purpose, a unity of will. And this is the kind of love that we, too, are called to share in, a love that wishes the other to grow and to be free to take their own way, make their own choices.

And what has that to do with the Incarnation? If we go on emphasizing the point that creation and incarnation are facets of the same nature of God at work, we will see that, just as God creates us to be 'in God's image', to be free, adult, responsive and responsible sharers in God's love and God's work, so the Incarnation does the same. Faced with the image of God in human form, Jesus, showing us what we are called to be, we choose. We choose whether to recognize ourselves, our family likeness, or to deny it. Where we deny it, there is the crucifixion, and yet the resurrection constantly re-presents us with our choice again.

This is all in danger of sounding dangerously binitarian, about the Father and the Son, but it is not. Creation, recreation and sanctification are all the work of the three persons. Father, Son and Holy Spirit all create and recreate in us the possibility of seeing what we are called to be, of growing into that likeness in which we are made. And the continuing love of the three persons 'in themselves' reminds us what this is all for. Our goal is to be drawn into the life and love of God. God's love is such that it has room even for us, it is a love that wishes to include all that it has made.

Once again, the point at which this abstract-sounding statement makes most sense is at the Eucharist, and in prayer. In the Eucharist, we take Christ's body in order to become Christ's body. We become what we are made to be. Accepting the Father's gift and giving thanks to the Father, receiving the son's body so that we might become God's 'Sons', accepting the transforming work of the Holy Spirit, who makes bread and wine, body and blood, and who makes our own body and blood into the body of Christ, at that point we are truly taken into the life and love of the Trinitarian God. And at that point it is not just we, as individuals, who are there, but the whole communion of saints, past and present. A foretaste of the Kingdom of God.

Notes

1   For example, the Church of England produced two doctrine reports, one on 'God' and one on the 'Holy Spirit'. This seems a strange distinction to make.

2   The perfect example of this would be Jurgen Moltmann, whose early christological book, *The Crucified God* (SCM 1974), is breath-takingly original, in a way that *The Church in the Power of the Holy Spirit* (SCM 1977) is not.

3   A good place to pursue the Orthodox understanding of the Trinity is in V Lossky, *The Mystical Theology of the Eastern Church* (Eng. trans. 1957).

4   All these viewpoints represent positions adopted in the first few Christian centuries, but rejected as 'heretical'.

5   The baptismal formula, for example, appears almost universally as 'I baptize you in the name of the Father, the Son and the Holy Spirit' in early sources.

6   Augustine is nearly always taken out of his historical context and blamed for views that would have been shared by most of his contemporaries. Certainly, because his theology has been so vastly influential, he may be the one remembered to be responsible, but it hardly seems fair to expect him to be without historical conditioning.

7   The Orthodox solution, which is to say that both Son and Spirit proceed from the Father, is certainly very appealing, but it easily introduces a kind of hierarchy by the back door, in that 'Fatherhood' is made to be the prime substance of 'Godhead'.

8   *The Forgotten Trinity* 1 (BCC 1989), p. 6.

9   Cf. Janet Morley, *All Desires Known* (MOW/WIT 1988), cf. p. 19 'O God our

Mystery'. Cf also Brian Wren, *What Language Shall I Borrow?* (SCM 1989), p. 215, 'How Wonderful the Three in One'.

[10] *We Believe in God* (Church House Publishing 1987), ch. 7.

[11] This is good biblical stuff, though perhaps found particularly in Romans.

[12] I will not here enter into the difference between symbol and sacrament, except to say that I imagine the Eucharist is both.

[13] Catherine LaCugna, *God for Us* (Harper San Francisco 1991).

[14] Most of these reasons have to do with the classical 'grammatical' rules about what may appropriately be said of our knowledge of God. LaCugna has little sympathy with this approach.

[15] Moltmann abandons the distinction, cf. *The Trinity and the Kingdom of God* (SCM 1981), p. 160 'I found myself bound to surrender the traditional distinction between the immanent and the economic Trinity, according to which the cross comes to stand only in the economy of salvation, but not within the immanent Trinity.'

[16] Sally McFague, *Models of God* (Fortress 1987).

[17] Leonardo Boff, *The Maternal Face of God* (Collins 1989).